Princesses Get Bullied Too…

By: Jay'Lyn Chancellor

Annie was a very smart First Grader that all the children loved.

She was very nice and always there for her friends and family whenever they needed her.

After school on a Thursday evening, Annie's best friend Greg was walking home with her when he noticed a sign so he asked "Annie, there is a pageant coming to town, will you be in it?" "I'll ask my Mother", replied Annie.

After talking to her mother, Annie couldn't wait to get to school to tell Greg the great news; she was going to be in the local pageant.

Can you draw and color what you think the local pageant sign would look like?

On Friday, Annie and her Mother went out shopping for a very pretty dress. On Saturday morning, Annie did great in the pageant, she won!

Can you draw and color a picture of a very pretty dress that Annie can wear to the pageant? What color is the dress? _____

When Annie got to school on Monday, she told her classmates the good news of her win and how she was not afraid to be on the stage in front of many people.

*** Let's Talk***

1. Why do you think Annie is afraid to be on stage?

_____

_____

2. What do you think Annie friends said about her winning the local pageant?

_____

_____

3. What do you think will happen next?

_____

_____

Everyone in the class was so happy for Annie, except Josh.

Josh was not very friendly;

he liked to pick on the other students for doing good things.

*** Let's Talk ***

If Josh was your friend, what would you tell
him about the way he feels?

_____

_____

_____

_____

_____

_____

_____

_____

_____

By Friday, Josh was bullying Annie and saying things that were not very nice to her about winning a pageant.

This was the first time Annie experienced bullying so she was too afraid to tell the teachers or her mother.

She thought that if she told the teacher or her mother that they would get mad at her so she allowed Josh to hit her, tease her and call her names.

Can you draw and color a picture of Annie afraid? What advice would you give Annie?

_____

_____

_____

_____

One day, Annie came home from school upset. Her Mother asked her what happened at school but Annie was too afraid to tell her Mommy.

After a few hours she decided to tell her Mother. Her Mother was so proud of her for being able to tell her that this was going on at her school.

The next day, Annie's Mother talked to the teacher about the things that Josh was doing. The teacher talked to Josh about the things he had been doing and let him know that it was not nice.

The teacher also let Josh know that hitting, teasing, and not playing nice with the other children was not nice.

Can you draw and color a "No Bullying" sign for the school?

At first, Annie was too afraid to play with Josh again until she saw how nice he was being to the other children. Annie decided to play with Josh once again and he was very nice to Annie.

Josh told Princess Annie that he was sorry for being a bully which was not nice. They became the best of friends from that day forward.

If you were Annie, how would you handle these situations that you read in the book?

_____

_____

_____

_____

_____

_____